Sons not SERVANTS

Sons not SERVANTS

ROBERT MORRIS

STUDY GUIDE

ISBN: 978-1-951227-40-1 Paperback
ISBN: 978-1-951227-41-8 eBook

We hope you hear from the Holy Spirit and receive God's richest blessings from this book by Gateway Press. We want to provide the highest quality resources that take the messages, music, and media of Gateway Church to the world. For more information on other resources from Gateway Publishing®, go to gatewaypublishing.com.

Gateway Press, an imprint of Gateway Publishing
700 Blessed Way
Southlake, Texas 76092
gatewaypublishing.com

Printed in the United States of America
21 22 23 24   5 4 3 2 1

CONTENTS

SESSION **1**   The Robe of Righteousness 1

SESSION **2**   The Ring of Authority. 13

SESSION **3**   The Shoes of Sonship. 27

Leader's Guide. 41

THE ROBE OF RIGHTEOUSNESS

We are not sons because we serve. We serve because we are sons of God. We are sons because we know Jesus, not because of our behavior.

ENGAGE

What is the best gift you have ever received? What is the worst?

WATCH

Watch "The Robe of Righteousness."

- Look for the difference between what is earned and what is a gift.
- Watch for how God enables us to live as His children.

(If you are not able to watch this teaching on video, read the following. Otherwise, skip to the **Talk** section after viewing.)

READ

When I say we are sons, not servants, that does not mean we don't serve. We do serve, and we are servants of God. But we serve because we are sons; we're not sons because we serve. We are sons and daughters because of birthright, not behavior.

In this series of three lessons, we will look at the return of the prodigal son. When he returns, his father gives him three gifts: a robe, a ring, and shoes. Each of these gifts has a special meaning in Scripture.

In this passage in Luke 15, notice how many times you see the word *son* and the word *servant*.

> But when he came to himself, he said, "How many of my father's hired servants have more than enough bread, but I perish here with hunger! I will arise and go to my father, and I will say to him, 'Father, I have sinned against heaven and before you. I am no longer worthy to be called your son. Treat me as one of your hired servants.'" And he arose and came to his father. But while he was still a long way off, his father saw him and felt compassion, and ran and embraced him and kissed him. And the son said to him, "Father, I have sinned against heaven and before you. I am no longer worthy to be called your son." But the father said to his servants, "Bring quickly the best robe, and put it on him, and put a ring on his hand, and shoes on his feet. And bring the fattened calf and kill it, and let us eat and celebrate. For this my son was dead, and is alive again; he was lost, and is found." And they began to celebrate (vv. 17–24 ESV).

Hired servants means employees, not slaves. So we see that even the father's employees have more than enough.

In verse 19, the son says he is *no longer* worthy to be called "son," implying that in the past he was worthy. The son starts to make his point, but the father stops him before he can finish his request to be treated as a servant. The father tells his servants to bring a robe, ring, and shoes. Every one of these things is a gift you give to a son, not to a servant. It's what you take away from servants, but you give to sons. We see the distinction between servants and sons in passages such as John 8:35, Galatians 4:7, and John 15:15.

What is the robe? Isaiah 61:10 says,

> I will greatly rejoice in the Lord,
> My soul shall be joyful in my God;
> For He has clothed me with the garments of salvation,
> He has covered me with the robe of righteousness.

The robe represents righteousness. Righteousness means 'right standing with God.'

Earned or a Gift?

This will change everything in your life. So many of you will answer this question that righteousness is a gift, but you *live* as if it is earned. Understanding this will change everything about the way you see God and about the way you see yourself. Everything about your behavior and your performance. Everything about the way you see others. Everything about the way you treat others, treat yourself, and treat God.

Every gift you receive is 100 percent gift and zero percent earned. The prodigal son had done nothing to earn these gifts. Nothing. They were *gifts*.

When the son said, "I am no longer worthy," he was thinking that he *was* worthy at some point in the past. We think the same way sometimes. When you have a bad week, you think you're not worthy that week, but then you have a good week—you pray and study the Bible and read the devotionals—and that week, you are worthy. But the truth is that you have never been worthy. None of us is worthy. The prodigal son wasn't worthy when he was at home doing the right things. That is purely a performance mentality. It is the same for us today.

We could also ask whether righteousness is earned or *imputed*. Romans 4:6 says, "David also describes the blessedness of the man to whom God imputes righteousness apart from works." We see the same use of the word *imputed* in Romans 4:23-24; He imputes it to *us* as well. Imputes means that God balances our accounts. In Romans 4:3, the same Greek word is rendered as 'account.' When Abraham believed God, God put righteousness into Abraham's account. God balanced that by putting Abraham's sin into His Son's account. It is the same for us. The reason your account is balanced is because God took your debt out of your account and put His assets into your account.

We serve the Lord, but we have to serve from a son and daughter mentality. We are adopted into His family. Righteousness is a gift.

Don't Listen to the Accuser

> Then he showed me Joshua the high priest standing before the Angel of the Lord, and Satan standing at his right hand to oppose him. And the Lord said to Satan, "The Lord rebuke you, Satan! The Lord who has chosen Jerusalem rebuke you! *Is* this not a brand plucked from the fire?"
>
> Now Joshua was clothed with filthy garments, and was standing before the Angel.
>
> Then He answered and spoke to those who stood before Him, saying, "Take away the filthy garments from him." And to him He said, "See, I have removed your iniquity from you, and I will clothe you with rich robes" (Zechariah 3:1-4).

This Joshua is the high priest who led the Israelites back into the Promised Land after the exile.

In this passage from Zechariah, Satan is standing at Jesus' right hand to oppose Joshua. Jesus rebukes the accuser, removes Joshua's iniquity (filthy clothes), and replaces them with *rich robes*. Iniquity is from the root word inequity. What this means is that none of us is equal with God. And iniquity is not just the evil we do.

In the Garden of Eden, there was the Tree of Life and the Tree of the Knowledge of Good and Evil. So the choice is not between good and bad, but between death and life. Even the good things we have to offer God fall short. Isaiah 64:6 says, "All our righteousnesses *are* like filthy rags." The best thing about me is not as good as the worst thing about God.

He removes the iniquity, He rebukes the accuser, and finally in this passage in Zechariah, He robes us in rich robes. He doesn't leave us naked. In Revelation 3:18, He clothes His saints in white garments so that the "shame of your nakedness may not be revealed."

Live Like a Son/Daughter

Even though none of us is righteous (Romans 3:10), God has gifted us with the robe of righteousness to help us live righteously. Even though righteousness is a gift, I still have the choice to live like a son and live righteously in the world. God expects us to use that gift. Revelation 19:8 says that in heaven, we will be "arrayed in fine linen, clean and bright, for the fine linen is the righteous acts of the saints." We will be rewarded then for our righteous deeds on earth. When we are tempted to live unrighteously, the Holy Spirit will empower us. Even though it is not our performance that puts us in right standing with God, we should still want to be a good witness.

NOTES

_____

_____

_____

_____

_____

_____

_____

_____

_____

_____

_____

_____

_____

_____

_____

_____

_____

_____

_____

_____

_____

_____

TALK

These questions can be used for group discussion or personal reflection.

Question 1

The prodigal son had faulty thinking, believing he was worthy at some point in his life. Have you ever had faulty thinking about who you are in Christ? How has your thinking changed?

_____

_____

_____

_____

Question 2

Our heavenly Father is always looking for prodigals to come home. Think about how He welcomed you when you turned to Him. Who are some prodigals in your life you could encourage to turn to Christ?

_____

_____

_____

_____

Question 3

Read John 8:35. What are some of the differences between an employee (hired servant) and a son or daughter?

_____

_____

_____

_____

Question 4

Read Ephesians 2. What is God rich in? What changes in our positioning when we become believers?

_____

_____

_____

_____

Question 5

In what ways does Jesus act as our defender and intercessor?

_____

_____

_____

_____

PRAY

If studying alone, ask the Holy Spirit to reveal the truth about Himself to you. If in a group, take some time to pray for each other as you think about the truths discussed in this session.

EXPLORE

Do you want to go deeper with this teaching? Here are some additional things to think about, pray for, or write about in your journal throughout the next week.

Key Quote

> *We're sons and daughters because of birthright, and not behavior.*

How would you describe your birthright as a believer? How does that comfort you?

_____

_____

_____

_____

_____

Key Verses

Luke 15:17-24; John 8:35; 15:15; Isaiah 61:10; Zechariah 3:1-4; Revelation 19:8

What truths stand out to you as you read these verses?

_____

_____

_____

What is the Holy Spirit saying to you through these Scriptures?

_____

_____

_____

Key Question

How does knowing that righteousness is a gift change the way we see God, ourselves, and others?

Key Prayer

Father God, thank You for Your great mercy! Thank You for gifting us with robes of righteousness. We don't deserve Your love or mercy, but we are so grateful. Lord, we thank You for Jesus' sacrifice to save us. It's a debt we can never repay. We want to live righteously and honor You with our lives, our words, and our deeds. We praise You for the work You are doing to change hearts and lives. In Jesus' name, Amen.

2

THE RING OF AUTHORITY

All authority is delegated. The ring represents the authority of the one who gave it. Humility, faith, and obedience are the three traits tied to the ring of authority.

ENGAGE

Was there a time as a child when, after disobeying your parents, something funny or embarrassing happened to you?

RECAP

In the previous session, we learned that we are all sons of God because of what we believe, not because of anything we have done. Like the prodigal son, we may have thought we were worthy at some time; however, we can never be worthy. We receive God's free gift of mercy when we have faith. When we live as a son, we will help bring others to God.

How did your behavior this week reflect the love and grace of God to others?

WATCH

Watch "The Ring of Authority."

- Look for the three traits of authority.
- Consider how you can model the way Jesus exhibited those traits in your own life.

(If you are not able to watch this teaching on video, read the following. Otherwise, skip to the **Talk** section after viewing.)

READ

In Luke 15:22, the second thing the prodigal's father asks for the son is a ring. The ring represents authority in Scripture. This authority comes through God's grace, through faith.

Here are some Scriptures that demonstrate the ring of authority:

Then Pharaoh took his signet ring off his hand and put it on Joseph's hand; and he clothed him in garments of fine linen and put a gold chain around his neck. And he had him ride in the second chariot which he had; and they cried out before him, "Bow the knee!" So he set him over all the land of Egypt (Genesis 41:42–43).

You yourselves write *a decree* concerning the Jews, as you please, in the king's name, and seal *it* with the king's signet ring; for whatever is written in the king's name and sealed with the king's signet ring no one can revoke (Esther 8:8).

The ring represents the authority of the one who gave it. When you saw the ring on the hand of the prodigal son, you knew he had authority.

Years ago, I was a staff member and an elder at Shady Grove Church (which is now our Gateway Church Grand Prairie Campus). One Sunday, Pastor Olen Griffing was preaching, and he said, "When I was younger, I could stop an 18-wheeler with one hand." How was this possible? Pastor Griffing had been a Texas State Trooper. When he held up his badge with one hand, it demonstrated his authority. He got that authority from the State of Texas.

Luke 15 tells us the authority we have is a gift from the Father. When we're rebuking the enemy from our family, it's not our authority—it's God's authority.

Mark 1:22 tells us the people were astonished at Jesus' teaching, "for He taught them as one having authority." All authority is delegated. Romans 13:1 says, "All authority comes from God" (NLT). So the father in Luke 15 delegates authority back to the prodigal son. Likewise, as a son or daughter of God, how do we walk in that authority and how do we use that authority? There are three things that help us walk in authority. Jesus exemplified all three of these things.

Humility

The quickest way to lose authority is to walk in pride. Jesus showed up with humility.

Here are some examples of humility in others and the authority they had. Luke 9:1 tells us Jesus gave His disciples "power and authority over all demons, and to cure diseases." In Luke 10, He expanded that authority to 70 disciples, who were also new believers:

> Then the seventy returned with joy, saying, "Lord, even the demons are subject to us in Your name."
>
> And He said to them, "I saw Satan fall like lightning from heaven. Behold, I give you the authority to trample on serpents and scorpions, and over all the power of the enemy, and nothing shall by any means hurt you. Nevertheless do not rejoice in this, that the spirits are subject to you, but rather rejoice because your names are written in heaven."
>
> In that hour Jesus rejoiced in the Spirit and said, "I thank You, Father, Lord of heaven and earth, that You have hidden these things from *the* wise and prudent and revealed them to babes. Even so, Father, for so it seemed good in Your sight (vv. 17–21).

Jesus gave that authority to 70 disciples who were babes in the faith. Authority over demonic spirits was hidden from the wise and prideful. Babes who walk in humility will have authority in God's name.

Many years ago, when I was doing crusades with James Robison, I would sometimes be called upon to help deal with a demonic spirit that manifested in someone who had responded to the message. This was done offstage in a separate room. One time, I went to the room feeling very proud that I had been asked to bring deliverance, and I encountered a large, strong woman who was possessed. She was being held down in her chair by two men. As soon as I walked in, the woman threw those men off her and looked at me. Out of her mouth came a *deep* demon's voice, saying, "I've been waiting for you." I was scared to death and stood there frozen. All of a sudden, I heard a little voice say, "Stop it!" An elderly 97-pound woman over in the corner stood up to those demons. She pointed at the woman (addressing the spirit) and said, "You stop it right now. You stop talking, you stop making a scene, and you let this precious woman go, in the name of the Lord Jesus Christ and by the Word of God and by the blood of the Lamb." She walked up to the woman, put her hand on the woman's face, and said, "It's okay, sweetie. They're gone." And they were gone.

The elderly woman had authority because she walked in humility. I had no authority because of my pride.

Faith

Matthew 8:5–10 tells the story of Jesus and the centurion:

Now when Jesus had entered Capernaum, a centurion came to Him, pleading with Him, saying, "Lord, my servant is lying at home paralyzed, dreadfully tormented."

And Jesus said to him, "I will come and heal him."

> The centurion answered and said, "Lord, I am not worthy that You should come under my roof. But only speak a word, and my servant will be healed. For I also am a man under authority, having soldiers under me. And I say to this *one*, 'Go,' and he goes; and to another, 'Come,' and he comes; and to my servant, 'Do this,' and he does *it*."
>
> When Jesus heard *it*, He marveled, and said to those who followed, "Assuredly, I say to you, I have not found such great faith, not even in Israel!"

Note the word *also*. The centurion had great authority because he understood authority. He recognized that Jesus was under authority, and he had faith because he understood that.

I learned a lesson recently when my wife, Debbie, had an accident in the house and seriously cut several of her fingers on both hands. It came at a time when Debbie was also in the late stages of *both* the flu and shingles. She was expecting to be finished with the diseases on the next day, and then the accident happened. We took her to the emergency room for the third time in a month.

As we walked into the room, I thought, "Satan, why don't you fight like a man? Quit coming after my wife!" But then I wondered, *Why am I not able to cover her?* The Lord told me that I was believing two lies. The first lie was that this was just normal—flu, shingles, infections, etc. Second, the Lord showed me that I didn't quite understand warfare. He told me, "Yes, it's normal for the enemy to engage in warfare with My children, but it's *not* normal for them to lose. That's not normal".

God showed me examples from the Bible. The Egyptian army followed the Israelites, but they also drowned. Daniel was thrown in the lions' den, but God shut the mouths of the lions. And Shadrach, Meshach, and Abed-Nego were thrown into the fiery furnace, but they came out, and their clothes didn't even smell like smoke. All through Scripture there is warfare, but we win. The shield of faith— what you believe—quenches every flaming arrow of the evil one. Even I, as a pastor, had allowed myself to lose my faith by believing the wrong thing.

Obedience

Now when He came into the temple, the chief priests and the elders of the people confronted Him as He was teaching, and said, "By what authority are You doing these things? And who gave You this authority?"

But Jesus answered and said to them, "I also will ask you one thing, which if you tell Me, I likewise will tell you by what authority I do these things: The baptism of John—where was it from? From heaven or from men?"

And they reasoned among themselves, saying, "If we say, 'From heaven,' He will say to us, 'Why then did you not believe him?' But if we say, 'From men,' we fear the multitude, for all count John as a prophet." So they answered Jesus and said, "We do not know."

And He said to them, "Neither will I tell you by what authority I do these things.

"But what do you think? A man had two sons, and he came to the first and said, 'Son, go, work today in my vineyard.' He answered and said, 'I will not,' but afterward he regretted it and went. Then he came to the second and said likewise. And he answered and said, 'I *go,* sir,' but he did not go. Which of the two did the will of *his* father?"

They said to Him, "The first."

Jesus said to them, "Assuredly, I say to you that tax collectors and harlots enter the kingdom of God before you" (Matthew 21:23–31).

Jesus challenged the Pharisees about their question as to where He got His authority by asking them a "loaded" question about the baptism of John. When they couldn't answer Him, he told them the story of two sons (vv. 28–31).

What this story demonstrates is that *authority comes from doing the will of the Father.* Those same sinners that the Pharisees despised so much had the same authority Jesus had, because they obeyed. The Pharisees, on the other hand, said they would uphold the law, but they didn't. Those who obeyed were going to heaven before the Pharisees would.

Even as a believer, you can have a ring of authority, but you can walk in pride and have no authority. Or you can believe a lie and lose your authority. Or you can walk in disobedience and rebellion and lose your authority. The choice is up to you.

NOTES

_____

_____

_____

_____

_____

_____

_____

_____

_____

_____

_____

_____

_____

_____

_____

_____

_____

_____

_____

TALK

These questions can be used for group discussion or personal reflection.

Question 1

Jesus exhibited all three traits tied to wearing the ring of authority—humility, faith, and obedience. Can you give examples from Jesus' life where He displayed each trait?

_____

_____

_____

_____

Question 2

Have you ever experienced an encounter with a demonic spirit? How was it handled?

_____

_____

_____

_____

Question 3

Let's look at how the Israelites left Egypt. How did they show humility, faith, and obedience? How did God show His authority over their enemies?

_____

_____

_____

_____

Question 4

What are other biblical stories where people showed humility, faith, and obedience in the midst of a battle? How did God's authority triumph over their enemies?

_____

_____

_____

_____

Question 5

Do you have any personal testimonies of victories or failures with humility, faith, and obedience? How was your spiritual authority impacted?

_____

_____

_____

_____

PRAY

If studying alone, ask the Holy Spirit to reveal the truth about Himself to you. If in a group, take some time to pray for each other as you think about the truths discussed in this session.

EXPLORE

Do you want to go deeper with this teaching? Here are some additional things to think about, pray for, or write about in your journal throughout the next week.

Key Quote

> *When we're rebuking the enemy from our family, it's not our authority—it's God's authority.*

What are some ways that you might rebuke the enemy from your family?

_____

_____

_____

_____

_____

Key Verses

Luke 9:1; 10:1; 17–21; Genesis 41:42–43; Esther 8:8; Mark 1:22

What truths stand out to you as you read these verses?

_____

_____

_____

What is the Holy Spirit saying to you through these Scriptures?

_____

_____

_____

Key Question

What things can we do on a regular basis to help us remember who we are in God?

Key Prayer

Father God, thank You for calling us to be Your children and making us joint heirs with Christ. Thank You for the robe of righteousness and for the ring of authority. We repent for walking in pride, unbelief, and disobedience. Help us to remember who we are in You and to grow strong in the truth of Your Word. We love You, Lord. We praise You for the work You are doing. In Jesus' name, Amen.

3

THE SHOES OF SONSHIP

It is by grace, not by works, that we are sons and daughters of God. We must give up our rights so that God can restore them to us.

ENGAGE

How many pairs of shoes do you have in your closet?

RECAP

In the previous session, we learned that humility, faith, and obedience are necessary in order for us to exercise the authority God has given to us as His children.

Did you have a chance to be humble, faithful, or obedient in your interactions with others this week?

WATCH

Watch "The Shoes of Sonship."

- Look for what shoes represent to believers.
- Consider how we become sons of God.

(If you are not able to watch this teaching on video, read the following. Otherwise, skip to the **Talk** section after viewing.)

READ

The third thing the prodigal's father asked his servant to bring for his son was shoes. We're going to talk about what shoes represent in the Bible.

Take Your Shoes Off

In the Bible, shoes represent rights. The prodigal son did not believe he deserved rights as a son. That's why he wanted to become a hired servant. In the Bible, when you took your shoes off, it meant that you were giving up your rights.

We see this in several stories in the Bible. One of those is the story of Ruth and Boaz.

Boaz wanted to marry Ruth, but there was a closer relative who had the first right to marry her. This man was called the kinsman redeemer. Boaz asked him if he wanted to marry Ruth, but the kinsman redeemer said no.

> Now this *was the custom* in former times in Israel concerning redeeming and exchanging, to confirm anything: one man took off his sandal and gave *it* to the other, and this *was* a confirmation in Israel (Ruth 4:7).

It was the custom to take one's shoes off to confirm the agreement. The Law explains this in Deuteronomy in the context of a man who does not want to marry his brother's widow:

But if the man does not want to take his brother's wife, then let his brother's wife go up to the gate to the elders, and say, "My husband's brother refuses to raise up a name to his brother in Israel; he will not perform the duty of my husband's brother." Then the elders of his city shall call him and speak to him. But *if* he stands firm and says, "I do not want to take her," then his brother's wife shall come to him in the presence of the elders, remove his sandal from his foot, spit in his face, and answer and say, "So shall it be done to the man who will not build up his brother's house." And his name shall be called in Israel, "The house of him who had his sandal removed" (Deuteronomy 25:7–10).

Can you imagine this man's mortgage application a couple years later? First Name: The. Last Name: Removed. Full Name: The house of him who had his sandal Removed. You can imagine the reaction.

The first thing God told Moses to do at the burning bush on Mt. Sinai was, "Take your shoes off." To talk to God, you have to give up all your rights. The same thing happened to Joshua:

And it came to pass, when Joshua was by Jericho, that he lifted his eyes and looked, and behold, a Man stood opposite him with His sword drawn in His hand. And Joshua went to Him and said to Him, "*Are* You for us or for our adversaries?"

So He said, "No, but *as* Commander of the army of the Lord I have now come."

> And Joshua fell on his face to the earth and worshiped, and said to Him, "What does my Lord say to His servant?"
> Then the Commander of the Lord's army said to Joshua, "Take your sandal off your foot, for the place where you stand *is* holy." And Joshua did so (Joshua 5:13–15).

The Man is Jesus. He tells Joshua to give up his rights, as Jesus is the Commander of the Lord's army. The Israelites could not have defeated Jericho on their own. Immediately after this He gives the people the instructions to walk around the city seven days.

Put Your Shoes Back On

What you put on your feet when you put your shoes back on is your rights. Moses and Joshua put their shoes back on and led the people of Israel, but they led them under God.

There are many rights you receive as a child of God. One is power—the power to share the gospel. In Acts 1, the believers were filled with the power of the Holy Spirit to be witnesses and preach the gospel. Ephesians 6 says that part of our armor is to have our feet shod with the preparation of the gospel of peace.

Another right is authority. Jesus gives us authority over the enemy to tread on serpents and scorpions.

Freedom is another right. In 2 Chronicles 28, the people of Israel took some of the people of Judah captive, and the first thing they did was take the captives' shoes off. Eventually, when they were restored, Israel gave their shoes back.

This is the parable of the prodigal son, but there are two sons in this story. The older son refuses to come to the party after the father gives the prodigal son the robe, ring, and shoes. It is important for us to understand this.

> Now his older son was in the field. And as he came and drew near to the house, he heard music and dancing. So he called one of the servants and asked what these things meant. And he said to him, "Your brother has come, and because he has received him safe and sound, your father has killed the fatted calf."
>
> But he was angry and would not go in. Therefore his father came out and pleaded with him. So he answered and said to *his* father, "Lo, these many years I have been serving you; I never transgressed your commandment at any time; and yet you never gave me a young goat, that I might make merry with my friends. But as soon as this son of yours came, who has devoured your livelihood with harlots, you killed the fatted calf for him."
>
> And he said to him, "Son, you are always with me, and all that I have is yours" (Luke 15:25-31).

Verse 31 sums up the rights and benefits of sonship this way: the presence and the provision of God.

Jesus has just finished telling two parables: the parable of the lost coin (vv. 8-10) and the parable of the lost sheep (vv. 3-7). In both parables the people throw a party at the end, and Jesus says there is joy in heaven when one sinner repents. In order to understand the older son, we need to understand why Jesus told these parables in the first place.

> Then all the tax collectors and the sinners drew near to Him to hear Him. And the Pharisees and scribes complained, saying, "This Man receives sinners and eats with them." So He spoke this parable to them (Luke 15:1–3).

The Pharisees were mad that Jesus received sinners. Praise God that He receives sinners like you and me.

Jesus tells these three parables (which are really one parable) for two reasons. The first is to show how much the Father values people. The second reason is to show us that it is *all grace and not works*. Jesus constantly battled with the Pharisees about this fact. The Pharisees got angry about Jesus hanging out with sinners because they felt *they* had earned their relationship with God and the sinners had not. The older son represents the Pharisees, and the younger son represents sinners.

In Luke 18:9–14, Jesus tells a story about a Pharisee and a tax collector who go into the temple. The Pharisee thanks God that he is not like those other people (sinners). The tax collector, on the other hand, won't even lift his head but asks God for mercy. Jesus says the tax collector goes home justified with God rather than the Pharisee.

In Matthew 20:1–16, Jesus says the workers who come late into the vineyard—even at the eleventh hour—receive the same wages as those who were there the entire time. The workers who worked the whole day were mad that by their pay, the landowner had made the late arrivals equal with them. This is exactly how the Pharisees felt. They had worked harder. But Jesus says they get exactly the same thing as sinners: forgiveness for all their sins and eternity in heaven.

Going back to Luke 15:17—in all the years I have preached, I'd never noticed the word "hired" in "hired servants." A hired servant is an *employee*. When he gets his paycheck, he's earned it. But that's not what we are. We're not hired servants. We don't earn it with Jesus. We're sons and daughters, and it's a free gift from the Father. That's what the Pharisees couldn't stand—that the sinners had not earned it.

If you feel like you have earned your right relationship with God, then you will want others to earn it also. You'll look at others who don't live up to your standard of righteousness and be critical and judgmental. You'll be like the Pharisees. Christians can feel like they have earned their relationship with God through all their service and then be upset when attention is paid to a new believer.

In addition, if you make others earn their right relationship with God, then you'll make them earn their right relationship with *you too*. Many people get this when they're growing up, regard-less of the type of parents they have. They think, *When I act right, my parents love me. And when I don't act right, my parents don't love me.* We can project that same attitude onto God when we are adults—God loves us when we are good. But the truth is *God loves you whether you like it or not.* You can never change God's love for you.

This is my burden for the church. We are sons and daughters—completely and totally—by grace. We are not hired servants (employees). God doesn't owe us anything.

So there are three parables in Luke 15. In the parable of the lost coin, the woman searches for it until she finds it. In the parable of the lost sheep, the shepherd finds the lost sheep, puts it on his shoulders, and brings it back home. But in the parable of the prodigal son, the father *waits* for the son to return home. Why? Because the son is a person—not a coin or an animal. The son is a human who has a will, and he has to make his own decision to give up his rights. Even though the Father is waiting for you, you'll have to make the decision to give up your rights. Once you do, then the Father is with you, and all that He has is yours.

Also, you have to keep giving up your rights. You don't do it just one time. Like the apostle Paul, you die daily (see 1 Corinthians 15:31).

Not long ago I had a difficult time forgiving someone who had wronged me. The Lord told me I needed to forgive him. I knew that, but I kept arguing with God and insisted on having the right to be angry at him.

I even quoted Ephesians 4:26: "Be angry, and do not sin." According to the Bible, I have the right to be angry. But God reminded me of Galatians 2:20: "**I have been crucified with Christ**; it is no longer I who live, but Christ lives in me; and the *life* which I now live in the flesh I live by faith in the Son of God, who loved me and gave Himself for me" (emphasis added).

I am dead, and God is living in me, so I have given up all my rights. I have no right to be angry with other people because, even though my sins (and everybody's sins) put Jesus on the cross, God is not angry with me.

It's by grace; it's not by works. It's a gift; it's not earned. Salvation is not a goal to be achieved—it's a gift to be received. We're sons, not servants.

NOTES

_____

_____

_____

_____

_____

_____

_____

_____

_____

_____

_____

TALK

These questions can be used for group discussion or personal reflection.

Question 1

Read Luke 18:9–14. What are the differences between the Pharisee and the tax collector? With whom do you most identify and why?

_____

_____

_____

_____

Question 2

How does the belief that you can earn sonship lead to self-righteousness?

_____

_____

_____

_____

Question 3

Why do you think it can be difficult for us to see ourselves as sons and daughters of God?

_____

_____

_____

_____

Question 4

Have you ever experienced a "prodigal son" moment in your walk with God or with a loved one? If so, how has that experience affected your walk with God?

_____

_____

_____

_____

PRAY

If studying alone, ask the Holy Spirit to reveal the truth about Himself to you. If in a group, take some time to pray for each other as you think about the truths discussed in this session.

EXPLORE

Do you want to go deeper with this teaching? Here are some additional things to think about, pray for, or write about in your journal throughout the next week.

Key Quote

A hired servant is an employee. When he gets his paycheck, he's earned it. But that's not what we are. We're not hired servants. We don't earn it with Jesus. We're sons and daughters, and it's a free gift from the Father.

How do you view your relationship with God—through the eyes of a hired servant or a son/daughter?

_____

_____

_____

_____

_____

Key Verses
Luke 15:22, 25-31; Ruth 4:7; Deuteronomy 25:7-10
   What truths stand out to you as you read these verses?

_____

_____

_____

   What is the Holy Spirit saying to you through these Scriptures?

_____

_____

_____

Key Question
How can you adjust your behavior each day to reflect your position
as a son or daughter of God?

Key Prayer
   Lord, thank You for welcoming us as Your sons and daughters.
   Help us understand that we are Yours, not because of anything
   we've done but only by Your wonderful grace. We desire to follow
   You and obey You because we love You, Lord. Thank you for the
   overwhelming and amazing grace and mercy You offer us in the
   gift of salvation. Help us to walk with You as we go into our week,
   and may we bring Your presence, Your love, Your mercy, and Your
   grace to each person we meet. In Jesus' name, Amen.

LEADER'S GUIDE

The *Sons Not Servants* Leader's Guide is designed to help you lead your small group or class through the *Sons Not Servants* curriculum. Use this guide along with the curriculum for a life-changing, interactive experience.

BEFORE YOU MEET

- Ask God to prepare the hearts and minds of the people in your group. Ask Him to show you how to encourage each person to integrate the principles all of you discover into your daily lives through group discussion and writing in your journals.
- Preview the video segment for the week.
- Plan how much time you'll give to each portion of your meeting (see the suggested schedule below). In case you're unable to get through all of the activities in the time you have planned, here is a list of the most important questions (from the **Talk** section) for each week.

SESSION ONE

Q: The prodigal son had faulty thinking, believing he was worthy at some point in his life. Have you ever had faulty thinking about who you are in Christ? How has your thinking changed?

Q: Read John 8:35. What are some of the differences between an employee (hired servant) and a son or daughter?

SESSION TWO

Q: Jesus exhibited all three traits tied to wearing the ring of authority—humility, faith, and obedience. Can you give examples from Jesus' life where He displayed each trait?

Q: Let's look at how the Israelites left Egypt. How did they show humility, faith, and obedience? How did God show His authority over their enemies?

SESSION THREE

Q: Read Luke 18:9–14. What are the differences between the Pharisee and the tax collector? With whom do you most identify and why?

Q: Why do you think it can be difficult for us to see ourselves as sons and daughters of God?

SUGGESTED SCHEDULE

1. **Engage** and **Recap** (5 Minutes)
2. **Watch** and **Read** (20 Minutes)
3. **Talk** (25 Minutes)
4. **Pray** (10 minutes)

HOW TO USE THE CURRICULUM

The One Thing
This is a brief statement under each session title that sums up the main point—the key idea—of the session.

Engage
Ask the icebreaker question to help get people talking and feeling comfortable with one another.

Recap
At the first meeting, provide an overview of the curriculum and encourage everyone to read and prepare before each meeting.
For the following meetings, recap the previous session and invite members to talk about any opportunities they have encountered to apply what they learned.

Watch
Watch the videos (recommended).

Read
If you're unable to watch the videos, read these sections.

Talk
The questions in this curriculum are intentionally open-ended. Use them to help the group members reflect on Scripture and the truths learned in the session.

Pray

Ask members to share their concerns and then pray together. Be sensitive to the Holy Spirit and the needs of the group.

Explore

Encourage members to complete the written portion in their books before the next meeting.

KEY TIPS FOR THE LEADER

- Generate participation and discussion.
- Resist the urge to teach. The goal is for great conversation that leads to discovery.
- Ask open-ended questions—questions that can't be answered with "yes" or "no" (e.g., "What do you think about that?" rather than "Do you agree?")
- When a question arises, ask the group for their input instead of answering it yourself before allowing anyone else to respond.
- Be comfortable with silence. If you ask a question and no one responds, rephrase the question and wait for a response. Your primary role is to create an environment where people feel comfortable to be themselves and participate, not to provide the answers to all of their questions.
- Ask the group to pray for each other from week to week, especially about key issues that arise during your group time. This is how you begin to build authentic community and encourage spiritual growth within the group.

KEYS TO A DYNAMIC SMALL GROUP

Relationships

Meaningful, encouraging relationships are the foundation of a dynamic small group. Teaching, discussion, worship, and prayer are important elements of a group meeting, but the depth of each element is often dependent upon the depth of the relationships between members.

Availability

Building a sense of community within your group requires members to prioritize their relationships with one another. This means being available to listen, care for one another, and meet each other's needs.

Mutual Respect

Mutual respect is shown when members value each other's opinions (even when they disagree) and are careful never to put down or embarrass others in the group (including their spouses, who may or may not be present).

Openness

A healthy small group environment encourages sincerity and transparency. Members treat each other with grace in areas of weakness, allowing each other room to grow.

Confidentiality

To develop authenticity and a sense of safety within the group, each member must be able to trust that things discussed within the group will not be shared outside the group.

Shared Responsibility

Group members will share the responsibility of group meetings by using their God-given abilities to serve at each gathering. Some may greet, some may host, some may teach, etc. Ideally, each person should be available to care for others as needed.

Sensitivity

Dynamic small groups are born when the leader consistently seeks and is responsive to the guidance of the Holy Spirit, following His leading throughout the meeting as opposed to sticking to the "agenda." This guidance is especially important during the discussion and ministry time.

Fun!

Dynamic small groups take the time to have fun. Create an atmosphere for fun, and be willing to laugh at yourself every now and then!

ABOUT THE AUTHOR

Robert Morris is the senior pastor of Gateway Church, a multi-campus church in the Dallas/Fort Worth Metroplex. Since it began in 2000, the church has grown to more than 39,000 active members. His television program is aired in over 190 countries, and his radio program, *Worship & the Word with Pastor Robert*, airs on more than 850 radio stations across America. He serves as chancellor of The King's University and is the bestselling author of numerous books, including *The Blessed Life*, *Truly Free*, *Frequency*, and *Beyond Blessed*. Robert and his wife, Debbie, have been married 39 years and are blessed with one married daughter, two married sons, and nine grandchildren.

NOTES

More resources for your small group by Pastor Robert Morris!

Blessed Families Study Guide: 978-1-949399-55-4 DVD: 978-1-949399-52-3

Living in His Presence Study Guide: 978-1-945529-55-9 DVD: 978-1-949399-42-4

Lost and Found Study Guide: 978-1-945529-85-6 DVD: 978-1-949399-48-6

More Than Words Study Guide: 978-1-949399-65-3 DVD: 978-1-949399-66-0

REAL Study Guide: 978-1-945529-51-1 DVD: 978-1-949399-49-3

RELAT1ONSHIP Study Guide: 978-1-949399-54-7 DVD: 978-1-949399-51-6

The Blessed Life Study Guide: 978-0-997429-84-8 DVD: 978-1-949399-46-2

The End Study Guide: 978-1-945529-88-7 DVD: 978-1-949399-53-0

The God I Never Knew Study Guide: 978-1-945529-54-2 DVD: 978-1-949399-41-7

Why Am I Here? Study Guide: 978-1-945529-71-9 DVD: 978-1-949399-50-9

Words: Life or Death Study Guide: 978-1-945529-56-6 DVD: 978-1-949399-43-1

Beyond Blessed DVD + Discussion Guide: 978-1-949399-68-4

Eternity Study Guide: 978-1-949399-95-0 DVD: 978-1-949399-94-3

The Kings of Babylon Study Guide: 978-1-949399-98-1 DVD: 978-1-949399-97-4

A Way in the Wilderness Study Guide: 978-1-951227-01-2 DVD: 978-1-951227-00-5

Sons Not Servants Study Guide: 978-1-951227-40-1 DVD: 978-1-951227-42-5

God Is... Study Guide: 978-1-951227-37-1 DVD: 978-1-951227-39-5

3 Steps to Victory Study Guide: 978-1-951227-34-0 DVD: 978-1-951227-36-4

You can find these resources and others at
www.gatewaypublishing.com